WILD! Exploring Animal Habitats

CREATURES ON A TOWERING MOUNTAIN

Francine Topacio

PowerKiDS press.
New York

Published in 2020 by The Rosen Publishing Group, Inc.
29 East 21st Street, New York, NY 10010

Editor: Elizabeth Krajnik
Book Design: Reann Nye

Photo Credits: Cover Ibrahim Suha Derbent/Photodisc/Getty Images; Series Art Lidiia/Shutterstock.com; p. 4 907Shots/Shutterstock.com; p. 5 Joe McDonald/ Corbis Documentary/Getty Images Plus/Getty Images; p. 6 Galyna Andrushko/ Shutterstock.com; p. 7 FiledIMAGE/Shutterstock.com; p. 8 Federico.Crovetto/ Shutterstock.com; p. 9 (top) kavram/Shutterstock.com; p. 9 (bottom) Dave Allen Photography/Shutterstock.com; p. 10 Scott E Read/Shutterstock.com; p. 11 Frenchwildlifephotograher/Shutterstock.com; p. 13 critterbiz/Shutterstock.com; p. 14 MZPHOTO.CZ/Shutterstock.com; p. 15 Richard Seeley/Shutterstock.com; p. 17 PhotocechCZ/Shutterstock.com; p. 18 zahoor salmi/Moment/Getty Images; p. 19 pawopa3336/iStock/Getty Images Plus/Getty Images; p. 21 Chris Curtis/ Shutterstock.com; p. 22 Robert Crum/Shutterstock.com.

Library of Congress Cataloging-in-Publication Data

Names: Topacio, Francine.
Title: Creatures on a towering mountain / Francine Topacio.
Description: New York : PowerKids Press, 2020. | Series: Wild! exploring animal habitats | Includes glossary and index.
Identifiers: ISBN 9781725304482 (pbk.) | ISBN 9781725304505 (library bound) | ISBN 9781725304499 (6 pack)
Subjects: LCSH: Mountain ecology-Juvenile literature. | Mountain animals-Juvenile literature.
Classification: LCC QL113.T67 2020 | DDC 591-dc23

Manufactured in the United States of America

CPSIA Compliance Information: Batch #CSPK19. For Further Information contact Rosen Publishing, New York, New York at 1-800-237-9932.

CONTENTS

MOUNTAIN BASICS

Mountains are some of the **harshest** habitats on Earth. From the bottom of the mountain to the top, there are great changes in the **temperature**, weather, and which plants and animals live there. Even though mountains can be harsh habitats, many different plants and animals live there. The species, or kinds, of plants and animals depend on the elevation, or height above sea level.

Creature Corner

Denali National Park was created to protect Dall sheep from being overhunted. It was the first national park created to **protect** wildlife. Dall sheep are a species of bighorn sheep.

Only one species of amphibian lives in Denali National Park. The wood frog is small—only about 0.4 to 2.75 inches (1 to 7 cm) long. They make loud calls in the spring.

The tallest mountain in the United States is Denali Peak in Alaska, which is part of the Alaska Range. Denali is 20,310 feet (6,190 m) tall. Denali is home to many species of **mammals**, birds, and bugs.

MOUNTAINS EVERYWHERE!

Every **continent** on Earth has mountains. Some mountains are made when large pieces of Earth's crust called tectonic plates crash into each other. Volcanoes form other mountains. The mountains in one part of the world are very different from the mountains in other parts of the world.

Sequoia trees are the tallest trees on Earth. Sequoia National Park in the Sierra Nevada Mountains is home to hundreds of thousands of these beautiful trees.

The United States has three major mountain ranges. Each of these mountain ranges is different and has different wildlife. The Appalachian Mountains are short and mostly covered in trees. The Rocky Mountains are tall and have **distinct** seasons. The Sierra Nevada Mountains are shorter than the Rocky Mountains, but taller than the Appalachian Mountains.

ALTITUDINAL ZONATION

Altitudinal zonation is how mountains are broken down into different **ecosystems** or **zones** based on altitude, or elevation. As altitude changes, so do temperature, what the soil is made up of, how much moisture is in the air, and other things that affect which plants and animals can live at certain altitudes.

Creature Corner

The Alpine salamander is one of the rarest amphibians in the world. It was discovered in 1988 on the slopes of Monte Viso in the Alps.

The type of zones a mountain has depends on where the mountain is. A mountain in the Andes, top, won't have all the same zones as a mountain in the Appalachians, bottom.

The lowest zone of a mountain is the lowland zone. This zone is different based on its **climate**. The next highest level is the montane zone, which is covered in forests. The subalpine zone has fewer trees. In the alpine zone trees begin to disappear entirely. The nival zone, or snow zone, is covered in snow almost all year.

LOWLAND CREATURES

The lowland zones of mountains are home to a great number of creatures. On many mountains, some larger animals living in the lowland zone also live in the area surrounding the mountain. Other animals living in the lowland zone, such as deer, elk, and moose, **migrate** up the mountain to find food in the summer and back down in the winter. Predators such as wolves follow these **prey** animals.

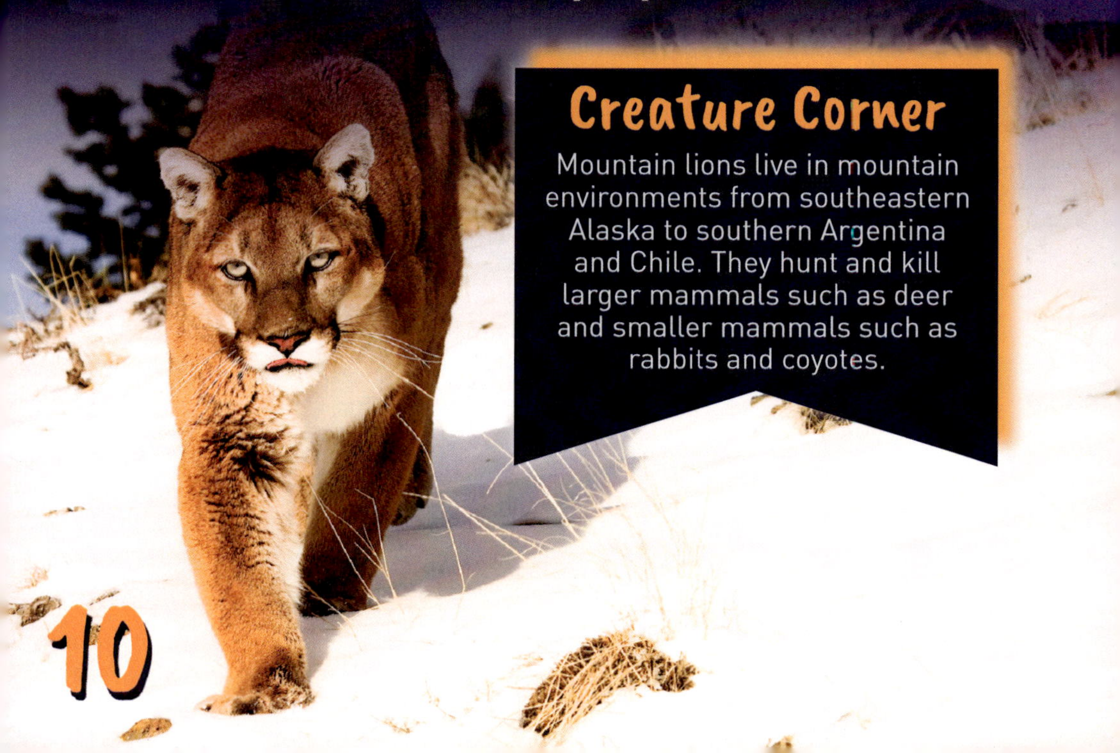

Creature Corner

Mountain lions live in mountain environments from southeastern Alaska to southern Argentina and Chile. They hunt and kill larger mammals such as deer and smaller mammals such as rabbits and coyotes.

Wolves have an important job in lowland habitats. They control the number of animals that eat grasses, such as deer and elk. This helps keep the habitat balanced.

Many different species of birds make their homes in the trees of the lowland zone. Small mammals such as squirrels and raccoons also call this zone home. Amphibians such as turtles and salamanders are found in the lowland zone, too.

AMERICAN BLACK BEAR

The American black bear is the most common and well-known bear species in North America. They live on and around mountains, usually in forests. Black bears are omnivores, which means they eat plants and animals. They eat whatever they can find, such as berries, fish, and even dead animals. They eat huge amounts of food in the summer and fall to store up fat for their winter sleep.

Black bears make a den to sleep in for the winter months. During this time, female black bears may give birth to two or three cubs. The cubs depend on their mother for everything until they come out of the den in the spring.

Creature Corner

Black bears aren't always black. They can be blue-gray, blue-black, brown, cinnamon, or even white! Cubs from the same litter can even be different colors.

Black bears often like to eat human food. If you're camping where black bears are known to live, don't leave food out for them to eat. They can get angry, though, so be extra careful!

MONTANE CREATURES

Creatures in the montane zone have **adapted** to life there. Some animals, such as snowshoe hares have white fur in the winter to blend in with their surroundings. In the summer, their fur is brown to match the grass and ground. This keeps them safe from predators such as foxes, weasels, and hawks. Others have thick fur to keep them warm. Others dig holes or find caves to shelter, or cover, them from the cold and weather.

Creature Corner

Marmots are large ground squirrels. They have small fur-covered ears, short thick legs, and claws they use to dig. They are found in many mountain habitats all over the world.

Pikas are small egg-shaped mammals that are in the same family as hares and rabbits. They live in the mountains of western North America and many parts of Asia. Pikas collect grasses to eat during the long winter.

The montane zone is also home to butterflies, honeybees, and hummingbirds that gather pollen and drink the nectar from wildflowers in the summer months.

THOUSANDS OF QUILLS

Porcupines are round, slow-moving **rodents**. They are known for their needlelike quills, which cover most of their body. A porcupine can have more than 30,000 quills. If an animal attacks the porcupine, its quills will come off in the animal's skin. When a porcupine is scared, its quills stand straight up.

Porcupines are herbivores, which means they only eat plants. There are two main groups of porcupines: New World Porcupines, which live in the western hemisphere, and Old World Porcupines, which live in the eastern hemisphere. Some kinds of porcupines live in burrows or in small caves. Others live in trees.

Female porcupines give birth to one to four babies at a time. The babies are born with soft quills that get harder over time.

WAY UP HIGH!

Life way up high isn't easy. The sun is strong, it's hard to breathe, the wind blows hard, there's little food, and there aren't many places to hide. However, you'll find life if you know where to look. Yaks, alpacas, and mountain goats have thick fur to keep them warm.

Creature Corner

Male markhors fight each other to be able to have babies with a female. They try to throw each other off steep cliffs. If one falls, a snow leopard will bring the markhor back to its den to eat.

Andean geese live high in the Andes Mountains in South America. They are large, with black and white feathers, a red bill, or mouth, and orange legs and feet.

Snow leopards have thick coats and long bushy tails that they curl around themselves when they sleep to keep warm. Their big paws help them climb the mountain's rocky slopes. Snow leopards hide in the rocks to catch their prey. They like to eat ibex and markhor, which are types of wild mountain goats.

SPLIT HOOVES

In the Rocky Mountains, bighorn sheep live high on the rocky slopes. They have adapted split hooves with rough bottoms to help them climb the mountain's steep cliffs and balance. Their hooves help them climb high to get away from predators. They also have good eyesight to make sure they don't fall.

Male bighorn sheep are known for their large curved horns, which they use to fight each other. The bones behind their horns are extra thick to keep the sheep from hurting their head. Males, called rams, live together. Females, called ewes, live together with their young. Rams and ewes only come together to mate, or to make babies.

Rocky Mountain bighorn sheep have horns that are, on average, more than 3.3 feet (1 m) long. Female bighorn sheep don't have horns this long.

PROTECTING MOUNTAIN HABITATS

Even though animals living in mountain habitats are highly adapted, they're not safe from human activities. People might hurt wildlife. Climate change, or change in Earth's weather caused by human activity, is melting the snow and ice on mountaintops. It also causes wildlife to climb higher to find shelter and food. People cut down trees for firewood, to make paper, for building, and to make room for farmland. This takes away homes for many different species.

If you visit a mountain habitat, remember that the creatures there are important. Mountain habitats are easily affected by even the smallest actions. Make sure you stay on marked paths and pick up your litter.

GLOSSARY

adapt: To change in order to live better in a certain environment.

climate: The average weather conditions of a place over a period of time.

continent: One of the seven great masses of land on Earth.

distinct: Easy to notice or understand.

ecosystem: A natural community of living and nonliving things.

harsh: Unpleasant and difficult to accept or experience.

mammal: Any warm-blooded animal whose babies drink milk and whose body is covered with hair or fur.

migrate: To move from one place to another to find food, have babies, or as the seasons change.

prey: An animal hunted by other animals for food.

protect: To keep safe.

rodent: A small, furry animal with large front teeth, such as a mouse or rat.

temperature: How hot or cold something is.

zone: An area that is different from other areas in a particular way.

INDEX

WEBSITES

Due to the changing nature of Internet links, PowerKids Press has developed an online list of websites related to the subject of this book. This site is updated regularly. Please use this link to access the list: www.powerkidslinks.com/wild/mountain